Poetry

2007

by
6th grade students of
Fairfield Middle School

1st WORLD
LIBRARY
Literary Society

Poetry 2007

by 6th grade students of Fairfield Middle School

© 1st World Library - Literary Society, 2007
1100 North 4th St. Fairfield, Iowa 52556
• Tel: 641-209-5000 • Fax: 641-209-3001
• Web: www.1stworldlibrary.com

First Edition

LCCN: 2007941969

SoftCover ISBN: 978-1-4218-9840-7
eBook ISBN: 978-1-4218-9841-4

Foreword

A balanced language arts curriculum provides instructional time for reading, speaking and writing. Reading is often given priority, but these components of literacy are all extremely important: as students develop their skills in one area, they enhance their proficiencies in the others. Sixth graders have opportunities to explore a variety of genres or categories in each area. They read fiction, nonfiction, poetry and biographies. They practice effective speaking by writing and delivering speeches about themselves and what they are learning.

This book is about writing and the writing process. Writing provides opportunities to clarify thinking, to learn to convey thoughts and emotions with precision and to reflect on what has been learned. Sixth graders write responses to what they read. They write and edit stories, research reports and opinion essays. They also read and write different kinds of poetry. This genre helps them learn to choose a particular word or phrase that not only fits, but expresses their point of view or creates a specific image. They develop the ability to write poetry and at the same time

1

become better thinkers, readers and writers.

Seeing their writing in print, particularly in a form that can be read by friends, family and teachers, motivates students to share what they think, know and understand. A book like this is about the sharing of experience. We hope you will enjoy reading the poems, and perhaps even find the opportunity to talk with the authors about the experience of writing them.

Margaret Kelly,
Director of Curriculum
Fairfield Community School District

Introduction

The poems you are about to read were written and selected by sixth graders of the Fairfield Middle School in Fairfield, Iowa. These eleven- and twelve-year-olds were exposed to a wide variety of poetry throughout the year. Students read, chanted, sang, rapped, acted-out, interpreted, memorized, and recited poems from famous authors. They also learned how to write many different types of poems, including Japanese tanka, haiku and magazine haiku, acrostic, bio, cinquain, color poems, concrete, couplets, diamanté, holiday poems, limericks, ocean research, and title down poems. The poems in this book are the culmination of what they learned. Some are funny, clever, creative, and silly, while others are serious or sad; yet all convey the thoughts and emotions of these young, budding writers. I'm proud of their work and willingness to share this personal side of themselves with others. Happy reading!

Ann Gookin,
6th Grade Language Arts Teacher
Fairfield Middle School

Haiku (hi'koo) Poetry

A traditional Japanese verse, written in 17 syllables divided into three unrhymed lines made up of five, seven, and five syllables, often on the subject of nature or the seasons.

Iowa

Iowa's grasslands
Are like an ocean of grass
When wind is blowing.

Darrin Dimmitt

Sun

Bright in the morning
Gets higher every hour
And falls down again.

Adam Mueller

Palm trees swaying while
Having fun in the bright sun
Dropping coconuts

Claire Slechta

The Blazing Sun

The sun is blazing
Everything is very hot
Shade is very scarce.

Ben Singer

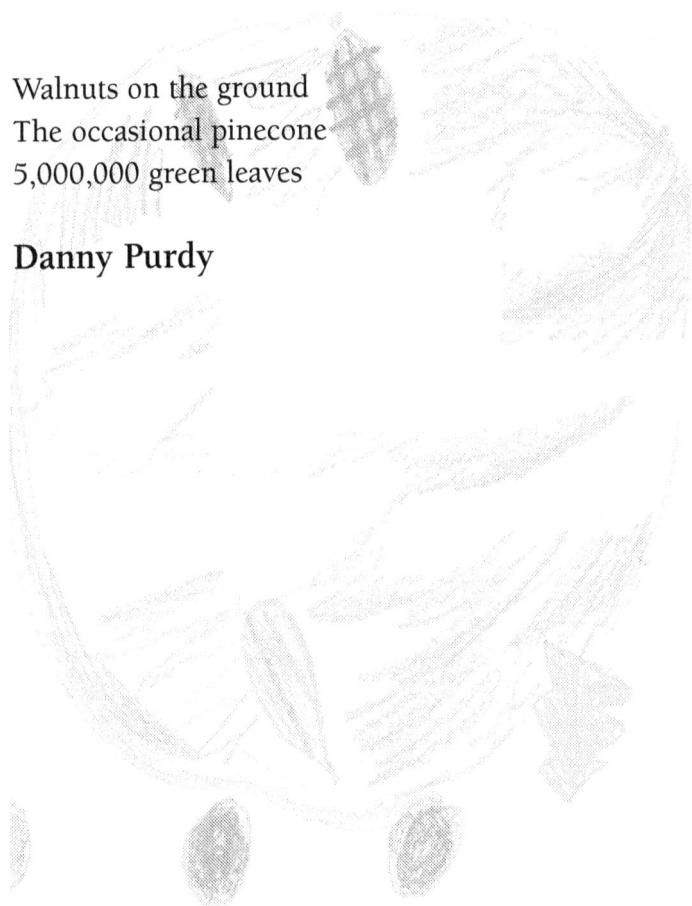

Walnuts on the ground
The occasional pinecone
5,000,000 green leaves

Danny Purdy

Magazine Haiku (hi'koo)
Poetry

We put a spin on the traditional Japanese verse by
adding inspirational pictures from magazines
and using them as our subject.

Baseball

Catching is for me
Not every ball is caught
Most of them will be.

Dusty Odell

My corn has gone mad.
Maybe I made it go mad,
Just very bad corn.

Forest Miller

Game Night

Games are so much fun,
Taboo, Cadoo, any will
do. You want to play?

Erin Thompson

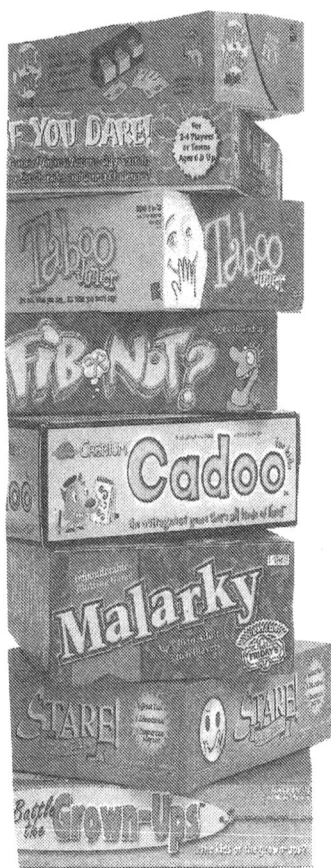

Shopping

I love to go shop
I like to shop and spend my
Mom's and dad's money.

Lacey Lankford

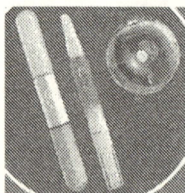

Elmo

I like how Elmo
laughs. I like to tickle him.
Elmo is funny.

Diana Sanchez

Yamahas

Yamahas are fast
180 when you floor it
Brake it and skid it.

Matthew Kaufman

Color Poetry

A poem written about a favorite color,
using the five senses:

Taste, touch, smell, sight and sound.

This poem is packed with imagery and metaphor.

Red

Red is Honda colors and fire trucks
And very hot.
Red is the taste of tomatoes on a salad.
Embarrassment makes me feel red.
Red is the sound of sirens, and the crackling of fire.
Red is apple farms, professional racing,
and a boiler room.
Riding in a fire truck is red.
Red is Valentine's Day.

Jacob Adam

Blue

Blue is dolphins and blue jays and wet.
Blue is the taste of blueberry pie.
Near the ocean makes me feel blue.
Blue is the sound of waves and rain.
Blue is an aquarium, airplanes, and the beach.
Blue is windsurfing.
Blue is a calm color.

Anna Topping

Orange

Orange is basketballs and oranges
and hot like lava from a volcano.
Orange is the taste of Hooters hot wings.
Sunburns make me feel orange.
Orange is the sound of the General Lee's
horn and meteoroids
flying through the sky.
Orange is Hooters, Harley Shops, and the Core.
The sun beating down so hard is orange.
Orange is orange chicken fresh and hot.

Dalton Cook

Green

Green is forest trees and leaves
and rough like old leaves.
Green is the taste of green apples.
Grasshoppers make me feel green.
Green is the sound of mowing lawns
and eating pickles.
Green is a rain forest, greenhouses,
green lakes and rivers, too.
Playing baseball in the grass is green.
Green is the best Kool-Aid.

Tyler Cooksey

Chrome Blue

Chrome blue is cars and oceans
and smooth like paint.
Chrome blue is the taste of blueberries.
Sleeping makes me feel chrome blue.
Chrome blue is the sound of waves
and a honking horn.
Chrome blue is car shops, paint shops,
and Wal-Mart.
Driving a go-kart is chrome blue.
Chrome blue is driving a 4–wheeler.

Makena Dettmann

Neon Red

Neon red is Kasey Kahne's car and sunburns
and smooth like metal.
Neon red is the taste of cherry cheesecake.
Getting embarrassed makes me feel neon red.
Neon red is the sound of firecrackers
and people cheering.
Neon red is in the #9 car, fire stations, and Mars.
Going to a race is neon red.
Neon red is hot like lava.

Ashley Henkel

Green

Green is infields and outfields
and leafy and smooth.
Green is the taste of pizza and Mountain Dew.
Sports make me feel green.
Green is the sound of crunching and cheers.
Green is baseball fields, football fields,
and wrestling mats.
Sliding in grass is green.
Green is the green monster.

Josh Dimmitt

Blue

Blue is ocean and sky and cold ocean waves.
Blue is the taste of blueberries.
Sad, lonely, and tired makes me feel blue.
Blue is the sound of rain and jazz.
Blue is the sky, the lake, and swimming in a pool.
Swimming with friends is blue.
Blue is the water smell.

Tyler Gilmore

Neon Red

Neon red is fire, lightning, and blazing hot fire.
Neon red is the taste of jalapeños peppers.
Going fast makes me feel neon red.
Neon red is the sound of an electric guitar
and a blasting stereo.
Neon red is the Cyclones, Chiefs,
and the Boston Red Sox.
Street racers are neon red.
Neon red is lightning.

Trey Downing

Green

Green is dirt bikes and grass
and bumpy green leaves.
Green is the taste of sweet grapes.
When I fall and touch the ground I feel green.
Green is the sound of a cool night with wind
blowing and meadows.
Green is gas stations, dinosaurs, and shirts.
A bruise is green.
Green is a kiwi.

Kyle Ford

Blue

Blue is the ocean and sky and smooth as water.
Blue is the taste of Gatorade.
When I'm sad makes me feel blue.
Blue is the sound of ocean waves and rainstorms.
Blue is a blueberry bush, a water slide,
and a swimming pool with friends is blue.
Blue is calm.

Luis Giron

Red

Red is roses and blood and runny.
Red is the taste of strawberries.
Mad makes me feel red.
Red is the sound of car crashes and fire drills.
Red is a fire station, McDonalds, and hospitals.
Angry is red.
Red is a fire truck.

Justin Hammes

Neon Green

Neon green is bright green grass,
the color that glows at night,
and slimy as gooey melted spearmint gum.
Neon green is the taste of sour green apples.
Excitement makes me feel neon green.
Neon green is the sound of our winning team, Kurtz
Dozing, and bright green trees swaying
back and forth in the wind.
The smell of a flower shop, a rainforest,
and Las Vegas with all that money is neon green.
Walking into the woods is neon green.
Neon green is so wonderful and bright like me.

Nichole Helmick

Blue

Blue is the sky and the ocean and smooth
under the water.
Blue is the taste of blueberry juice.
When I am sick makes me feel blue.
Blue is the sound of ocean waves and waterfalls.
Blue is when I go to the ocean.
Blue is swimming and diving into the pool.
Happiness is blue.
Blue is fresh air and smells good.

Maria Jimenez

Red

Red is a rose and a fire truck and
rough as a rose's thorn.
Red is the taste of cherries.
When I'm angry makes me feel red.
Red is the sound of a scream and a red alert.
Red is a firehouse, a fireplace,
and an ambulance ride.
Sunburns are red.
Red is a Christmas light.

Adam Mueller

Orange

Orange is basketballs and basketball rims
and rough like oranges.
Orange is the taste of buffalo wings.
Mad makes me feel orange.
Orange is the sound of the General Lee's horn
and the Trojan fight song.
Orange is Harley shops, Hooters,
and Grand Slam Sports.
Winning a game is orange.
Orange is like the smell of oranges.

Spencer Peterman

Blue

Blue is the big sky and the ocean water
and the fast rushing water.
Blue is the taste of nasty mushrooms.
Sitting in the house on a nice summer
day makes me feel blue.
Blue is the sound of the tuba and the violin
playing together.
Blue is the big beach, the big, big sky,
and a hot summer day.
Blue is Jolly Ranchers.

Britany Kopp

Green

Green is grass and trees and slippery.
Green is the taste of candy.
Happiness makes me feel green.
Green is the sound of radios and bubbles.
Green is nature parks, rainforests and coral reefs.
A quiet day is green.
Green is fresh paint.

Rachel Buelow

Neon Orange

Neon orange is caution cones and safety vests
and smooth as a cone.
Neon orange is the taste of sweet oranges.
Neon orange is the sound of dump trucks
and cymbals.
Neon orange is a wrestling meet, a basketball game,
and a construction site.
Dodge Chargers are neon orange.
Neon orange is marking paint.

Wyatt Aplara

Diamanté
(dee-*uh*-mahn-**tey**)Poetry

Diamante is a form of unrhymed poetry,
made up of 7 lines, the shape of a diamond. It begins
and ends with nouns of opposite meaning, and is written as a
comparison. Lines 2 and 6 use adjectives to describe the nouns,
and lines 3 and 5 use action verbs. The middle line 4 is the
magical line, where the subject gradually transforms
from one meaning to another.

Cubs & Cards

Cubs
Amazing, winners
Fielding, running, hitting
Great, super, awful, terrible
Missing, swinging, losing
Boring, losers
Cardinals

John Danielson

Sports
Fun, active
Moving, running, jumping
Games, balls, T.V., food
Sleeping, boring, sitting
Non-active, game systems
Lazy

Seth Davisson

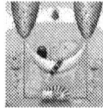

Boys & Girls

Boy
Tough, cool
Running, laughing, biking
Male, dad, female, mom
Skipping, giggling, jumping
Makeup, clothes
Girl

Trey Downing

Love and Hate

Love
Sweet, happy
Kissing, hugging, holding hands
Boys, family, enemies, strangers
Crying, frightening, lying
Hurtful, madness
Hate

Nichole Helmick

Summer & Winter

Summer
Hot, sunny
Splashing, sweating, playing
Vacation, water, ice, snow
Freezing, trembling, shaking
Cold, dull
Winter

Rachel Buelow

Dog & Cat Diamante

Dog
Fun, playful
Running, jumping, playing
Energetic, loyal, fluffy, mischievous,
Cuddling, purring, attacking,
Warm, cute,
Cat

Brianna Redmann

Diamante

P.E.
Hot, difficult
Running, throwing, kicking
Mile, fitness, teachers, quiet
Studying, reading, working
Boring
STUDY HALL

Lucas Story

Title Down Poetry

A poem that vertically tells a story,
using the letters of its title.

Soccer

Scraping your knees
Out in the sun
Carrying your body
'Cross the field
Energy flowing
Right through my veins

Kayla Septer

Cats

Cats are nice
And
Touching on a gloomy day

Austin Blomme

Iowa

In this state we love
Our Hawkeyes
With Herky, Ferentz
And new coach Lickliter!

Sidney Baumann

Rainbow

Red, blue, yellow, green,
All the colors I can see
In the sky so beautiful,
Now the sun shines down
Bringing out a brighter light
On this truly wonderful sight
Wondering where it leads.

Rachel Buelow

Baseball

Being outside having fun
Awake out in the field
Sun beating down on your head
Early in the morning, sun shining so bright
Being eager to bat
Apple smells in the air
Longing to make you sweat
Long time out in the field, hoping to have
some fun

Ryan Gaumer

Family

Family brings love
And joy from
Mothers and fathers
In the
Lives of their
Young

Tori Keltner

Shoes

Slick and shiny
Happily sitting on the shelf
Oh these are cute
Every girl loves shoes
Showing off my new shoes

Stephanie Kirby

Dog

Digging holes in the yard,
Oddly trying to catch its tail,
Goofing off some more.

Erin Kritenbrink

Dreamy Dream

Dozing off into a
Radical world of
Everyone's land of
Amazing things that
May not be mankind.

Jessica Lamb

Smile

Seeing someone
Making a funny face,
Incredible big teeth,
Laughing away,
Enjoying the moment.

Erin Thompson

Duck

Diving
Under the water
Crackers are its favorite food
Kwak it goes

Cole Vorhies

Penguin

Powerful
Energetic
Nice
Grand
Undetected
Intelligent
Never wrong

Gabe Bishop

Acrostic (*uh*-kraw'-stik) Poetry

A short poem in which the initial letters of the lines, taken in order, spell a person's name.

Mason Haynes

Male
Anarchist
Sneaky
Optimistic
Never hyper

Hopeful
Angry
Young
Nap taker
Enthusiastic
Safe

Mason Haynes

Tanka (täng'*kuh*) Poetry

A Japanese poem consisting of 31 syllables in 5
lines, with 5 syllables in the first and third lines,
and 7 in the others.

Snow

Snowflakes on the ground
Falling slowly down and down
White and beautiful
But now water on the ground
Freezing like never before.

Alyssa Chatfield

Fruity Tanka

There are lots of fruits
Apples, bananas, and more!
Each taste different
Fruity, juicy, or tangy
I love many kinds of fruit!

Erin Thompson

Sports

Sports are really fun
Like football and basketball.
Baseball is fun, too.
I could play sports all day long,
Even if it is nighttime.

Patrick Ives

Tanka

I love to climb my
Tree so high up in the air
And over the sky.
I love the sun striking down
On me shining so brightly.

Tori Keltner

Summer Falls

Waterfalls rain down
When it gets to the bottom,
It splashes away.
It flows away gracefully
When the summer falls awake.

William McCarroll

Flowers

Look at the flowers
They are so smooth in the wind
Gracefully swaying
Red and pink are their colors
Beautiful flowers swaying.

Kayla Septer

Tanka

Riding a dirt bike
I like going very fast
I hope I don't wreck.
Riding off very big jumps
Coming down is not so fun.

Dillon Fry

Concrete Poetry

A poem that visually conveys the poet's meaning through the graphic arrangement of letters, shapes, words, or symbols on the page.

Wyatt Aplara

UGLY

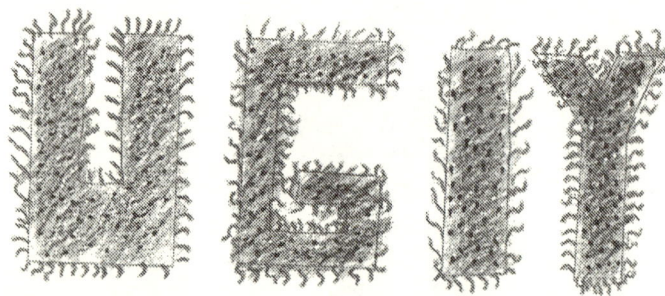

Tamicka Burks

84

bring

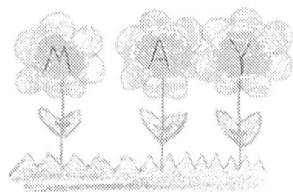

Erin Thompson

Hot dog in bun

Cool cat

Deven Hahn

I need one friend

I need two friends

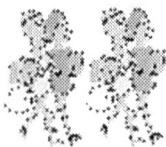

I need three friends

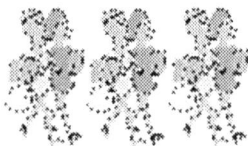

I need four friends

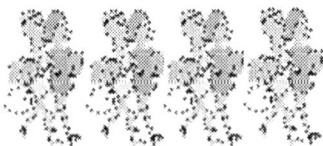

I need. . .

Kyle Hunter

Claire Slechta

Bio Poetry
(bi'o)=life

A poem about one's life.

Bio Poem

Kristen
Friendly, tall, busy, curious
Youngest child of Tim and Keeta
Lover of basketball, broccoli, and softball
Who feels tired after school, silly at softball games,
  happy at tae-kwon-do
Who needs a black belt in tae-kwon-do, a cell phone,
  and a new home phone
Who fears having a big sister and a cousin in the
  same grade as me
Who would like to see the ocean, my sister win the
  lottery, and my brother not find a girlfriend
Resident of Fairfield; West Jefferson
Terrell

Kristen Terrell

Ocean Poetry

Our sixth graders at F.M.S. study an oceanography
unit in science where they research and find ten
facts about a living animal or plant from the ocean.
In language arts class, students use their research
facts to create a poem.

Mean Killer

I'm the mean killer whale.
My mate gets up to 23-33 feet.
I, on the other hand, get up to 15-20 feet long.
You will find me in deep or shallow waters
within 500 miles of land.
I hunt for fish, squid, birds, turtles, seals, sea lions,
otters, walruses, penguins, and other killer whales.
I'm black and white and have a big fin on my back.
My scientific name is Orcinus orca.
We can swim alone or we can swim in pods
of 3 to more than 20.
The boys can be identified by their
paddle-shaped flippers.
I'm the top predator of the ocean.
Our diets vary from one region to the other.
When hunting a large whale,
we may attack from several angles.

Britany Kopp

Graceful Swimmer

I am a bottlenose dolphin
I can save a human
From a great white shark
Even when it is dark.
My body is shiny, smooth, and sleek
And I am strong, not weak.
I live in the pelagic zone
I dislike being alone,
So I swim with my friends
The fun never ends.
I can be trained to do flips
And getting kisses on the lips.
Look! I can see my reflection!
Just making sure I look like perfection.
I then dine on squid and fish
Don't eat me, they wish.
I have the largest brain for my size
I don't have a disguise.
I like to be myself
Not like everyone else.
I am a bottlenose dolphin.

Nohema Graber

I Am the Sea Urchin

My scientific name is Sphaerchius granularis.
I live in the sea, yep, that's me.
I'm purple and white.
Don't step on me, for you will feel a pain in your foot.
I live in rocky sea beds and coral reefs.
I eat algae and organic debris.
My biggest enemy is the sea otter.
I say, please, don't eat me.
I am classified as an echinoid, an invertebrate.
I move by moving my spines, which I have a thousand.
I am the Sea Urchin.
I live in any sea, any ocean, and tidal pools.
I also have another enemy, the rainbow wrasse eats me.
Please, oh please, I beg of thee, don't eat me,
For I am the Sea Urchin, so small, but bold.
I'm an expert on me, for I am the purple Sea Urchin.

Rabbah Jones

Columns

48 inches high
Dendrogyra cylindricus
72 inches wide
Dendrogyra cylindricus
Tall stacks
Dendrogyra cylindricus
Covered with polyps
Dendrogyra cylindricus
Tiny creatures
Dendrogyra cylindricus
The size of
Dendrogyra cylindricus
A pencil eraser
Dendrogyra cylindricus
Eating plankton
Dendrogyra cylindricus
And small fish
Dendrogyra cylindricus
Being eaten
Dendrogyra cylindricus
By crown-of-thorns
Dendrogyra cylindricus
Drupella and parrotfish

Dendrogyra cylindricus
Found in reefs
Dendrogyra cylindricus
Commonly inhabited
Dendrogyra cylindricus
By spiral-gilled tube worms
Dendrogyra cylindricus
A massive species
Dendrogyra cylindricus
Cousin to
Dendrogyra cylindricus
The jellyfish
Dendrogyra cylindricus
And the sea anemone
Dendrogyra cylindricus
A skeleton of limestone
Dendrogyra cylindricus
I'm stuck in one place
Dendrogyra cylindricus
Why don't I stop saying that?
Because I won't
For that is who I am
Dendrogyra cylindricus
The pillar coral.

Olin Knight

Thresher Shark

I am the Thresher Shark.
I am black and blue and grey.
I am a popular game fish.
I chase school fish and sometimes squid.
I like cold pelagic waters far off coast.
I am usually 2.0-6.0 meters long.
I swim fast through the water.
My long, whip-like tail sets me apart
from other sharks.
I am the Thresher Shark.

Dillon Laughlin

Beautiful Blue Linkia

I'm a beautiful blue Linkia.
I live in the coral reefs.
I love to eat the algae from the rocks.
I float gracefully through the water.
I have five arms.
I am afraid of the giant triton for he might eat me.
I am a very peaceful star fish,
So please don't eat me!

Brianna Redmann

Black Spines

I am the spiny dogfish.
My scientific name is
Squalus acanthius.
I am about 1 meter long,
And you won't be able to find me
Unless you can swim 900 meters
Down in the ocean at cool water temps.
I eat schooling and bottom-living fish and
Can live up to 70 years.
I can't breed until I am at least 20 years old and
I'm often caught as salmon.
My scales aren't poisonous, but can infect
You with slimy bacteria.
I have a cousin named the lesser-spotted dogfish.
You can tell us apart by my lack of anal fin.
My nickname is spur dog or piked dogfish.
I thrash and I squirm to catch my prey.
I am the spiny dogfish.

Dalton Smith

A Giant Mystery

I be sixty feet long,
And fifteen hundred feet down.
Squigglin' my ten tentacles all around.
I be starin' at you,
With my big ol' eyes.
I'm just like a normal squid,
but double double supersized.
I be movin' through any ocean,
With the fins on my head.
Lookin' for some fish to eat,
Maybe squid instead.
Remember this: Giant Squid's the name.
Hiding in the ocean is my game.

T. J. Wood

Under Water Wiggle Worm

I am the tube worm
My colors are red and white
Day or night.
I am skinny
Not Winnie.
I live in the Pacific
That is very specific.
I live deep in the ocean
With not much commotion.
I eat tiny bacteria
But not Siberia.
I don't move
By anything else but the groove,
And this is my rap.

Ben Singer

Limerick (lim'er-ik) Poetry

A humorous, five-lined poem with an a-a-b-b-a rhythm & rhyme, using one couplet and one triplet.

Billy Bob

Poor Billy Bob had the flu
He kept making the noise, "Ah-choo!"
Sneezed once and twice
His mom gave him rice
Poor Billy Bob, oh, boo hoo.

Cierra Bielinski

Tim's Tomato

Tim found a tomato on the ground
He thought it would be fun to pound.
Got in a fumble
Fell with a grumble.
Now he was in the mound.

Cierra Bielinski

Limerick

There once was a boy named Ed
Who wanted to make a bed
He thought for a day
But started in May
So he kept his old one instead.

Katie Anderson

Limerick

There once was a man named Lee
Who went diving into the sea
He found a clam shell
Locked up in a cell
But he can't find the key.

Rachel Buelow

Limerick

There once was a girl named Hannah
Who one day went to her nana's
But when she walked she fell
Then it started to swell
Then she moved to Louisiana.

Hannah Christensen

Off the Board

There was a diver named Rufus Potter,
Who could dive like an otter,
He did a triple back-flip,
Performed perfectly without a slip,
But the pool had absolutely no water.

Spencer Dodd

My Limerick

There once was a girl named Bonnie
Whose two little legs looked scrawny
She tripped on a stump
And made a big thump
And went crying to her boyfriend, Ronnie.

Erin Thompson

Limerick

There once was a guy from New York
Who wanted to try some real pork
He went to the store
To see if they had a boar
Then his wife said that he was a dork.

Ashley Henkel

Grace Wants to Race

One of my friend's name is Grace
Who really wanted to have a race
She liked to holler
And be a bother
Until I said, "Okay!" to her face.

Nicci Mellott

Run in the Sun

I like to play in the sun
I also like to hop and run
Until one bright day
I fell into the bay
Now I think it's not that fun.

Nicci Mellott

My Sister

Every time I see my sister
All I notice is her blister
She always gets mad
Because I treat her bad
So she just calls for her mister.

Kimberly O'Carroll

The Girl Named Sara

There is this girl named Sara
She is so obsessed with her tiara
I tell her to stop
But she just spills her pop
So I ditched her for Kara.

Kimberly O'Carroll

Slim Jim

There once was a young boy named Jim
Who was bullied because he was slim
So one day he pigged out
And grew a tail and a snout
So the kids still make fun of him.

Olin Knight

My Limerick

Sometimes I go on dates
And sometimes I debate
But from what I can see,
He is looking at me
And I will go out late!

Grace Smith

Limerick

There once was a toad named Loat
Who had a very big boat
He was carrying a key
When he saw me
And he went onto a float.

Grace Smith

Pasture Poems
Inspired By Robert Frost

Famous American poet, Robert Frost, (1874 -1963), author of "The Pasture," inspired us when we read his old-fashioned poem. The following poems, written by our sixth graders, are updated interpretations of Frost's "Pasture" poem.

The Pasture

I'm going out to clean the pasture spring;
I'll only stop to rake the leaves away
(And wait to watch the water clear, I may):
I shan't be gone long.—You come too.

I'm going out to fetch the little calf
That's standing by the mother. It's so young,
It totters when she licks it with her tongue.
I shan't be gone long.—You come too.

Robert Frost

The Pasture

I'm going out to swim:
First I'll start out slow, then start sprints
Then my friends start to race to go get mints
I shan't be gone long.—You come too.

Sydney Howard

The Pasture—Part I

I am going out to ride the four-wheeler
I'll pop a wheelie
And will look silly
I shan't be gone long.—You come too.

Miranda Metcalf

The Pasture—Part II

I am going out to play softball
I'll hit a homerun
And play catcher in the sun
I shan't be gone long.—You come too.

Miranda Metcalf

My Pasture Poem

I'm going out to swim some laps:
I'll grow some muscles to show my peers,
The person who will happy is Mrs. Diers.
I shan't be gone long.—You come too.

Sage Richmond

My Pasture Poem

I'm going out to run some laps:
To work on my skills on the track,
Now I have an aching back.
I shan't be gone long.—You come too.

Sage Richmond

Pool

I'm going out to swim in the pool
I'll just do some laps,
And also a belly slap.
I shan't be gone long.—You come too.

Arwin Shrestha

Circus

I'm going out to the circus
To see some new tricks,
There might be people hit by bricks
I shan't be gone long.—You come too.

Arwin Shrestha

Couplets

A two-lined, often humorous poem
that ends in rhyme.

My Couplets

Around the corner I quickly sped
And through a light I realized was red.

There is a very smart snake
Who learned how to bake.

I found some spectacular tennis shoes
But I think they belong to a pack of kangaroos.

I drank a shake
While I waited for a cake to bake.

I wish I could use my pencil that is red
But I need a lot more lead.

I baked a loaf of bread
But somehow it turned out red.

That earthquake
Made me ache.

A mischievous boy named Blake
Threw a giant mud ball on Jake.

Clumsy Drake
Made the vase break.

That horrible fake
Put a steak in my shake.

T. J. Wood

Couplets

My classmate Kristen is really funny
When she goes home her mom calls her Honey.

My classmate Kim likes the color blue
And she thinks she is an owl hoo-hoo.

I have a paper route and it is long
Most of the time I get done at dawn.

My favorite animal is the monkey
But sometimes its name sounds really funny.

My classmate Dakota is very blond
We are still paying her jail bond.

My favorite movie is Nemo
Good thing he is not emo.

My dog Jack is really fat
When I told him he sat.

My best friend Jodi is very blind
And she has a very blank mind.

My dog Seth
Is very deaf.

Go ahead go get ready
While I call my friend at her wedding.

Alyssa Chatfield

Couplets

The moon sparkles at night
What a pretty sight!

Some girls
Like pearls.

April showers bring May flowers
Do they grow as tall as towers?

Smiling is so great
You do not feel any hate.

Glasses get wetter
Contacts are better.

My cat had fish
In her dish.

The glue
Was blue.

I can't wait until summer
Because school is really a bummer.

I don't like to beat my house
Because I have an annoying spouse.

My perfume is pink
It smells like candy, I think.

Nohema Graber

Holiday & Winter
Poetry

The Penguin

There once was a penguin that had no beak.
He tried to make a wish, but he couldn't speak.
He wrote a letter.
It fell in the shredder.
Then he became a really big freak.

Gabe Bishop

Penguin's Christmas

There once was a penguin that celebrated Christmas.
He had a friend that celebrated X-mas.
He thought it was lame.
He thought it was the same.
Then they found out they both played Tetras.

Gabe Bishop

Santa

Santa has a big red coat
He's chubby all around,
He slides down chimneys
Giving presents all around the town.
No one hears him on the roof
With his reindeer and his sleigh,
He only comes once a year
To children who are nice.
And I guarantee, if you are good and nice,
He will come to you.

Santa

Maria Clarken

Snow

Snow is white and fluffy
Sometimes icy and hard.
You can make all sorts of things
Making them is fun!
You can make a snow angel
Or snowballs for a fight.
You can make a big igloo
Or tunnels to crawl in.
All this snow can do
But there is a lot more!

Snow

Maria Clarken

Christmas Poem

Christmas caroling is something to do
But Santa keeps wondering what he's giving to you
I only want to sing
But when I sing, give them a big sting
I want to see presents under the tree
I also want to open one on Christmas Eve
There's nothing to do
But hope Santa comes to you.

Cole Emry

Christmas

I see shiny snow, crystal lights
I smell chicken soup and eggnog
I hear holiday songs and bells
I taste a lot of eggnog
I touch my presents when I open them

Christmas

Cole Emry

Christmas

Cocoa
Happy
Rudolph
Ice
Santa Claus
Toys
Merry
Angel
Star

Gabe Jaquez

Sledding

Sledding fast on down the hill,
It's the perfect kind of thrill.
Sliding left and sliding right,
Gliding through a snowball fight.
I hit a ramp, I touch the sky,
Then I learned that I can't fly.
Soon I landed with a "thump,"
I could feel a great big bump.
Upon my head, it hurt so much.
Then in fear I had to clutch.
My sled, for I could clearly see,
That I had landed in a tree.

Olin Knight

Hockey

I'm running, sliding, skating fast; I'm trying not to fall.
But I just can't control myself and then I hit the wall.
I get back up, but then I prove that I'm just out of luck.
For right then I got hit by a flying hockey puck.

Olin Knight

www.ingramcontent.com/pod-product-compliance
Lightning Source LLC
Chambersburg PA
CBHW031850090426
42741CB00005B/425